10 Bears in my Bed

This is Peter's Book

10 Bears in my Bed

A Goodnight Countdown by
Stan Mack

Pantheon Books

So they all rolled over
and one **flew** out.

So they all rolled over
and one **galloped** out.

So they all rolled over
and one **skated** out.

So they all rolled over
and one **roared** out.

So they all rolled over
and one **chugged** out.

So they all rolled over
and one **jumped** out.

So they all rolled over
and one **bounced** out.

So they all rolled over
and one **pedaled** out.

So they all rolled over
and one **tootled** out.

So one rolled over
and he **rumbled** out.

There were **none** in his bed

so the little one said ...

From his pictures for *The ABC of Bumptious Beasts* to those in *The Brownstone* ("Easy to look at, to listen to, to read, and to smile over." *Library Journal*), Stan Mack's comical characters are growing increasingly familiar to picture book audiences.

He has also created a prize-winning film for The Children's Television Workshop and co-authored as well as illustrated *One Dancing Drum,* selected by *The New York Times* as among the best of 1972.

Based on an old counting song, *10 Bears in my Bed* provides a happy way to help banish bedtime fears.

Library of Congress Cataloging in Publication Data   Mack, Stanley. 10 Bears in my bed.   SUMMARY: One by one the bears leave the bed until there are none.   [1. Counting out rhymes]   I. Title.   PZ8.3.M17Be   398.8   74-151   ISBN 0-394-82902-6 ISBN 0-394-92902-0 (Lib. bdg.)